Winston Churchill

by Harriet Castor
Illustrations by Lynne Willey

FRANKLIN WATTS
LONDON • SYDNEY

First published in 2000
by Franklin Watts
This edition 2002

Franklin Watts
96 Leonard Street
London EC2A 4XD

Franklin Watts Australia
56 O'Riordan Street
Alexandria, Sydney
NSW 2015

ISBN 0 7496 4363 3 (pbk)

A CIP catalogue record for this book is available from the British Library

Dewey Decimal Classification
Number: 941.084

10 9 8 7 6 5 4 3 2 1

Series Editor: Sarah Ridley
Historical Consultant: Barbara Searle

Printed in Great Britain

Winston Churchill

One winter's night in 1874, a boy was born in a duke's palace. The boy was the duke's grandson and his name was Winston Churchill.

In those days, many children in wealthy families did not see their parents much. Winston was looked after by a nanny. He called her 'Woomany', and loved her dearly.

But when he was seven, Winston was sent away to school. He was miserable, and often came bottom of his class.

Winston's father wanted Winston to be a lawyer, but he didn't think Winston was clever enough. So instead, when Winston left school, he trained to be a soldier.

He loved it, and was very good at battle tactics. In his spare time, Winston read as many books as he could. He knew he wouldn't be a soldier forever.

When Churchill was 24, there was a war in South Africa called the Boer War. Churchill had taken a break from the army, so he went to the war as a reporter.

One day, the train Churchill was travelling on was attacked. He took charge, and helped the wounded soldiers get to safety. Then he returned to the fighting and was captured.

By Jove! Who is that man?
Drive on. You can do it!

Thrown into prison, Churchill was desperate to escape.

He had no compass, no map and no money but he did get away. He hid on a coal train, and then down a mine.

At last, he reached safety. By now, everyone had heard about his bravery.

Churchill knew what he wanted to be: a politician, like his father. When he came back to Britain, he stood for election and won.

At this time, the two main political parties were the Conservatives, or Tories, and the Liberals. Churchill was a Tory. Soon, though, he began to disagree with what the Tory Government was doing. He decided to change parties.

Meanwhile, Churchill had fallen in love with Clementine Hozier. He wanted to ask her to marry him, but he was too shy.

At last he plucked up the courage.
And Clementine said yes.

By now the Liberals were in power. Churchill was put in charge of the navy. He was worried that there might soon be a war, so he worked hard to get the navy ready, just in case.

Churchill was right. In 1914 the First World War broke out when Germany attacked France. The British army was sent to help the French. Though he hated war, Churchill loved tackling a crisis.

Churchill was always trying to think up plans that would bring the war to an end. One plan was for an attack on Turkey, which was Germany's friend. The attack failed, and lots of men were killed.

Though several people had made the plan, everyone blamed Churchill. He was forced to leave his job.

Churchill decided to become a soldier again. Friends offered him safe jobs, but he wanted to join the fighting. He went to France, where most of the fighting was happening.

Conditions were horrifying, and thousands were dying. Churchill threw himself into organising and encouraging his men.

What Churchill really wanted was another job in Government. At last, he was made the Minister in charge of weapons and war equipment.

The Ministry workers didn't want Churchill as their boss. But soon he won them over. He worked so hard that he often slept at his office.

In 1918, the war ended. During the 1920s and 1930s, Churchill had a difficult time. He lost an election, and for a while he was out of a job.

Then, when he was elected to Parliament again, he started disagreeing with the Liberals. He decided to swap back to the Tory party.

During this time, Germany had been taken over by Adolf Hitler and his followers, the Nazis. Churchill thought that Hitler might start a war, and that Britain should get ready.

But the Government wanted to save money. Getting the army, navy and air force ready for war was too expensive.

Churchill wanted the Government to make an agreement saying that countries would help each other if Hitler attacked them. In 1938, Hitler invaded Austria. But Britain didn't help.

Next, Hitler was going to invade Czechoslovakia. Churchill wanted Britain to say this would mean war. But the Prime Minister, Neville Chamberlain, thought that by being friendly towards Hitler, war could be avoided.

I have had a meeting with Herr Hitler. There will be no war.

In 1939 Hitler invaded Poland. Finally, Britain did declare war. The people who had made fun of Churchill now realised he had been right.

Churchill was put in charge of the navy again. A signal was sent to all the ships: "Winston is back."

In 1940 Neville Chamberlain resigned. Churchill became the new Prime Minister.

Churchill had always been brilliant at making speeches. Now he went on the radio to tell everyone that things would be very difficult, but that Britain would win the war.

Hitler's army marched into France. Now Britain was fighting alone.

Everyone thought Hitler would invade Britain next. Cities and towns were bombed by German planes every night, but the Royal Air Force fought back.

Thousands of people were killed in the bombing raids. Churchill and his ministers met in underground War Rooms, for safety. Often Churchill visited the bombed areas.

To win Britain needed America's help. Churchill tried to persuade the American President to join the fighting. It was only when America was attacked that the President agreed.

In 1943 plans began for a British and American army to land in France and drive the Germans back. Churchill knew that this would be dangerous

but he was determined to win the war. The invasion, known as D-Day, took place in June 1944. The final stage of the war had begun.

During 1945, British planes bombed German towns and cities and in May, Germany surrendered. All over Britain the streets filled with people celebrating.

But there was still lots of work for Churchill to do. There was going to be an election. Churchill was popular, but he was tired and his campaign went badly. He lost the election.

Churchill was very disappointed, but he carried on working hard. He was still the leader of the Tories. And he began writing his war memoirs.

Six years later the Tories won another election. At almost 77 years of age, Churchill was Prime Minister again.

Now, though, many people thought he was too old.

At last, when he was 80, Churchill did give up being Prime Minister. He carried on making speeches and working on his books, though.

In 1965, at the age of 90, Churchill died. As his coffin travelled down the River Thames, people gathered to pay their respects. Many felt Britain had lost a great leader.

Further facts

The Holocaust

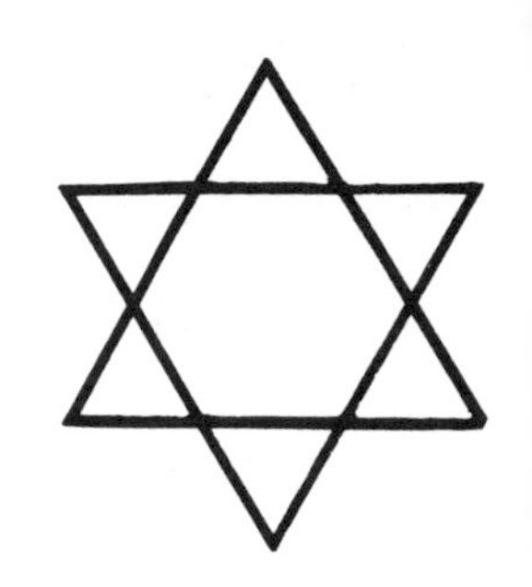

Hitler didn't just want to invade other countries. He had a much more terrible plan: he hated Jews, and he wanted to kill them all. Between 1938 and 1945 six million Jews were killed by the Nazis. This is known as 'the Holocaust'. Churchill called it "probably the greatest and most horrible crime ever committed in the whole history of the world."

Enigma

During the Second World War, the Nazis sent messages using a very complicated system of codes, made by a machine called 'Enigma'. In England, a large team of people secretly set to work trying to break these codes. After years of work, they finally did break the codes. This amazing achievement saved many British lives.

Churchill's rooms

After the Second World War, the Cabinet War Rooms in London, used by Churchill and his ministers, were kept just as they were. You can still visit them today.

Some important dates in Winston Churchill's lifetime

1874 Winston Leonard Spencer Churchill is born in Blenheim Palace, Oxfordshire.

1893 Churchill begins his military training.

1899 Churchill is captured during the Boer War (1899-1902) in South Africa. He escapes.

1900 Churchill is elected as MP for Oldham.

1904 Churchill leaves the Conservative Party and becomes a Liberal.

1908 Churchill marries Clementine Hozier.

1914-18 The First World War. Churchill is First Lord of the Admiralty, and later fights on the Western Front, in France.

1924 Churchill stands for election as a 'Constitutionalist', and later returns to the Conservative Party.

1939-45 The Second World War. Churchill is in charge of the Admiralty again, then in 1940 becomes Prime Minister.

1945 A General Election is called. The Conservative Party loses.

1951 The Conservatives win a General Election, and Churchill becomes Prime Minister.

1955 Churchill resigns as Prime Minister.

1965 Churchill dies, aged 90.